MARK
SHAND

ELEPHANT TALES

PENGUIN BOOKS

PENGUIN BOOKS

Published by the Penguin Group. Penguin Books Ltd, 27 Wrights Lane, London
w8 5TZ, England. Penguin Books USA Inc., 375 Hudson Street, New York, New
York 10014, USA. Penguin Books Australia Ltd, Ringwood, Victoria, Australia.
Penguin Books Canada Ltd, 10 Alcorn Avenue, Toronto, Ontario, Canada M4V 3B2.
Penguin Books (NZ) Ltd, 182–190 Wairau Road, Auckland 10, New Zealand · Penguin
Books Ltd, Registered Offices: Harmondsworth, Middlesex, England · These
extracts are from *Travels on My Elephant* by Mark Shand, published in Penguin
Books 1992. This edition published 1996. Copyright © Mark Shand 1991. All rights
reserved. The moral right of the author has been asserted · Typeset by Rowland
Phototypesetting Ltd, Bury St Edmunds, Suffolk. Printed in England by Clays Ltd,
St Ives plc ·
10 9 8 7 6 5 4 3 2 1

CONTENTS

Touch-me-not

Overnight, as if somebody had simply pushed a button, the monsoons left us, hurrying their black clouds further south. There was a distinct change in the air. It was crisp, alive; the early morning a few degrees colder and then warming as the sun rose. Autumn in India had arrived, bringing with it long, hot, golden days of harvest, celebration and festivals.

As instructed by Bhim (our mahout, or elephant-driver), we were to be on the look-out for the mimosa plant, otherwise known as 'Touch-me-not'. If you caressed its small, fern-like leaves they closed quickly, like a shutting book. The plant was an essential ingredient in the *puja* that was soon to be performed, where I would take on Bhim as my guru. Bhim called it the 'full-control ceremony'. Once Tara had eaten the blessed offering of mimosa and *gur*, he explained, she would be as obedient as a lamb and I would become the complete master. I was sceptical about this – not that I doubted Bhim, but because I doubted my abilities in controlling Tara, who was becoming friskier as each day passed. All the same I eagerly scanned the countryside for this plant. I was going to need all the help I could get. I was also encouraged by watching Gokul. He had apparently undergone a similar ceremony before we had started at Nandankanan and now was riding Tara with all the ability of a seasoned mahout, urging her along with shrill, squeaky cries.

We were well into rural Orissa, where fresh droppings were

abundant, signalling that we had entered elephant country. At the top of the giant bamboo groves ringing the paddy fields were tree houses, constructed like large storks' nests, access to which was gained by long, rickety ladders. These were anti-elephant *machans*, in which the villagers would sit at night and, by means of fireworks, crackers, shouting and flaming torches, attempt to deter rampaging beasts from demolishing their crops. In one village, where we stopped for tea, a young man, the local teacher, approached me.

'It is indeed,' he said, 'a wonderful thing that you are coming today. A gift from the gods.'

'*Namaste*,' I replied, delighted by this welcome but slightly bewildered.

'You, of course, will stop and help us?' he inquired eagerly.

'Well, yes,' now completely bewildered. 'If I can.'

'It is the tusker, sir. It has decimated our crops. It has already killed eleven of our people. You,' he said pointing to Tara, 'will catch it with your elephant.'

'Catch it with my elephant?' I answered amazed. Tara was happily rummaging around by the side of the tea-stall in search of food. The thought of the four of us with Tara engaged in some mad Mela Shikar chasing a highly dangerous elephant was absurd, and yet it was wonderful that he imagined it as being so simple. 'I'm sorry. You see we are just travelling through your beautiful country and we are not equipped to undertake such a task. Can't the government do anything about it?'

'The government,' he replied crestfallen, 'will do nothing. The tusker has only killed eleven people, sir. It must kill twenty-four before they are even considering taking actions.'

This was but one of many similar situations that I would encounter on my travels concerning the growing imbalance in India between the rural man and the natural life of the elephant living in harmony. Both are blameless and both are victims of greed; greed caused by the desire for timber, and the consequent massive deforestation. Elephants are creatures of habit. They have, for centuries, followed the same migratory routes in search of food. They arrive and find none: their larder has been cut down, and in desperation they turn to raiding crops on which the villagers' livelihood depends. The villagers are helpless and, even if they could afford to buy modern firearms, would usually be loath to use them. The elephant is a revered beast. Even when, which is seldom, a licence is granted to shoot an elephant that has been established as a rogue, more often than not the kill is not carried out. They revert to modern methods of trying to drug the animal, which in reality is an expensive and impractical situation. In a local newspaper I had read about a problem tusker that had killed and was causing havoc in another area of Orissa:

Licences were issued to kill it. When the hunters took position closer to the pachyderm to shoot him, they found that tears flowed from his eyes and he was supplicant. They dropped their plans and the tusker returned to the forests. The experts are of the opinion that the best way to tackle the situation is to capture the pachyderm. For every untoward incident created by the animal, they contend, there has been enough provocation by the timber merchants and the others who depend on the forest produce. The Minister for Forests, who was informed of the case, vehemently opposed all proposals to kill the elephant. He asserted that he would instruct the forest staff to have him tranquillized and deported to the zoo where necessary arrangements with Rs 1 lakh would be made to get him trained under an expert mahout from Assam.

Sadly, this situation is worsening. The Indian elephant is simply running out of living space. Recently a herd of thirty were creating havoc as close as twenty miles from Calcutta. It is fervently to be hoped that desperate measures like culling will not be introduced, and it is up to man to redress the balance. The tiger, which until recently was almost extinct, is beginning to make a dramatic recovery thanks to the resources and expertise made available to 'Project Tiger'. The elephant must now be given the same attention.

At Mandahat, we came to a mighty river, the Brahamani. Some people had told us authoritatively that it was six feet deep and could be crossed, while others shook their heads, knowledgeably stating that it had burst its banks. The latter were right: no one could ford it. We took a short cut along a road which would lead us to another bridge at Kabatobandah, where we hoped to meet up with a jeep. The road soon turned into a track, and then into nothing, as we found ourselves among fields choked with *baysharam*, a kind of bush with long wavy stems sprouting lilac, bell-shaped flowers, also known as 'shameless' for its gregarious, prolific and deep-rooted growth. It is considered a virulent weed which causes the Indian farmer enormous difficulties. The *baysharam* gave way to bamboo groves that had been decimated by wild elephants. In turn the bamboo led into sal forests still being decimated by human beings, in which the sound of a falling axe was always audible.

Considering their size, it is remarkable how elephants can move so soundlessly. Tara's footsteps, at their loudest, resembled the shuffle of an old man wearing carpet slippers. Because of this quietness, we encountered everything with an element of surprise, whether animal, human, bird or insect. Aditya was particularly happy. When we saw the flash of a golden oriole, a beautiful yellow bird with a jet-black streak through its eye dipping away with a raucous *cheeugh*, or the long ribbon-like tail of a paradise flycatcher, he would jot down his sightings excitedly in a small book. At one point Tara disturbed a carpet of big yellow butterflies that exploded into the air. A single butterfly, more courageous than its companions, attached itself firmly to the end of her trunk and after several vain attempts to dislodge it, by swinging it from side to side, she finally blew it off with a large sneeze.

The sal forests began to thin out and we moved carefully along the ridges dividing well-tended paddy fields. In corners of these fields were small tribal shrines situated under the spread of large shady trees. Dedicated to the goddess Devi, they consisted of groups of exquisite terracotta figures of horses, camels, elephants and bears, which were offered as gifts to the deity to ensure a healthy harvest to the indigenous Mundas. In the distance we heard the sound of drums. Spurring Tara on, we reached a small collection of thatched huts with pink walls surrounding a muddy courtyard where a Munda party was in full swing. A chain of men and women, dark, muscular people with full lips and handsome, high-cheekboned faces, were pounding their feet drunkenly in ankle-deep mud, performing a kind of ritual hokey-cokey.

At the sight of Tara looming over their compound, they threw their arms into the air, moaning loudly. The drum tempo increased, they whirled in ever-decreasing circles and finally collapsed, laughing, in an exhausted heap. A young woman wearing a brilliant azure sari, moulded to the contours of her body, untangled herself from the group and undulated over to Tara. She knelt gracefully and touched Tara's feet in obeisance. Each of her companions followed suit, and then offered us leaf cups containing a milky fluid which they had filled from large terracotta gourds. This was *handia*, a local rice beer. At first it tasted slightly bitter and fizzy, but after numerous replenishments, one was filled with a sense of contentment.

The drums started again. We were dragged to our feet and whirled round the compound. Now as drunk as our hosts, we proudly showed our paces. Aditya performed a sort of martial strut. I attempted to show them break dancing, which resulted in my head becoming firmly stuck in the mud, my feet waving in the air. Gokul, the professional, delighted the audience by doing somersaults, handstands and back flips. Even Tara, after draining one of the gourds, flapped her ears and shook her head while Bhim squatted with the elders and concentrated on the more serious aspect of things – drinking. When we took our leave the women presented us each with a frangipani flower, garlanded Tara and blessed us for a safe journey.

We reached a small river where a flash flood had washed away the bridge. A man sat forlornly on the bank drying out a bundle of soggy letters. He told us that while attempting to cross, he had been knocked over by the current and his bicycle was now caught in a bundle of branches in the middle of the whirling water. Bhim and Tara waded into the river. Directed by his sharp commands of '*Uhta, uhta,*' Tara lowered her trunk and plucked the bicycle from the branches as if it was a feather, depositing it gently in front of the grateful postman.

Out of curiosity, I penned a letter to myself in London and gave it to him. When I returned home three months later it was waiting for me. The letter was slightly the worse for wear, with an added message written on the back of the envelope. 'For Haathi-wallah from K. Rath, postman, thanking him sincerely.'

Guided by a full moon that washed the landscape in a pale light, we finally crossed the Brahamani over a long concrete bridge. It was late by the time we found the camp and by the look on Indrajit's face we knew there had been trouble between the two drivers.

'Khusto!' he spat fiercely. 'No good, he take rum. He always drunk. No helping either. I put tents, I cook, he does nothing. So I hit him. Either he go or I go.'

Aditya and I looked at each other in despair. We did not need a domestic squabble and we couldn't afford to lose Indrajit. He was invaluable. We checked the rum supply. Indrajit was right. Out of a new case of twelve bottles of rum one was missing. We found Khusto sitting in the jeep nursing a face that was even more swollen than usual. He mumbled something incomprehensible and turned his back to us insolently.

'Leave this to me, Mark,' Aditya said angrily.

For the next ten minutes there was an angry exchange of words punctuated by metallic slaps as Aditya banged his fist on the side of the jeep. It stopped abruptly. Khusto's voice had changed. He was now pleading. Eventually he shuffled into the firelight and muttered an apology to Indrajit and offered his hand. Indrajit took it hesitatingly and then with an angry smile touched him on the shoulder. The crisis it seemed was over for a time.

'What did you tell him?' I asked Aditya.

'Simple, my friend. He has stolen, so therefore he is a thief. I threatened to take him to the police station. That did it. I have told him that from now on Indrajit is the boss.'

'Do you think it will work?' I said.

'We'll see. Anyway, I don't think Khusto's bad, just foolish. He told me that all his problems stem from being born with too small a tongue.'

'What's that got to do with it?' I asked incredulously.

'I have no idea,' he laughed. 'Anyway we shall be without them for a few days. We are entering the forests of Daitari tomorrow and Bhim has announced that Tara is fit enough to carry the howdah.'

'What about my *puja*?' I insisted anxiously. 'Why can't we find this bloody mimosa plant?'

'Slowly, Mark, remember this is India.'

'Slowly indeed.' At this rate I was going to walk to Sonepur, I thought, as I finished my mug of coffee.

We were sitting round the fire which had been made in the crumbling porch of a deserted house near our camp. Bhim suddenly jumped to his feet and pointed into the dark confines of the house. '*Nag, nag!*' he cried excitedly. Everybody immediately disappeared and I was left sitting bewildered.

'What the hell's going . . . ?'

'Get out of there, Mark!' Aditya shouted.

'Will somebody tell me what's going on?'

'*Nag, nag!*'

'What in the hell is *nag*?'

'A snake, you idiot! Cobra!' Aditya yelled from the jeep, from which he, Bhim, Gokul and Indrajit reappeared armed with axes.

'Jeeesus! A snake! Oh, my God!' I shot out of the porch and fled towards Tara, who in the circumstances seemed to be the safest bet, noting on my way that Khusto had climbed on top of the jeep.

The boys advanced quickly into the house and a tremendous mêlée started. Shouts and screams followed by the sound of metal ringing on stone. I returned as nonchalantly as possible.

'Well?'

'*Nag* escape,' Bhim stated crossly. 'Big, maybe seven feet.'

'Seven feet!' I cried. 'Well, where is it now?'

'Maybe tent,' he leered happily. A thorough inspection of our sleeping quarters was made, but none of us slept well that night.

Early next morning, before setting off, Aditya and I took a detour to visit Bhuban, famous as Asia's most populated village. Our mission was more than one of tourism: we were to buy 'bombs', anti-elephant devices that Bhim said we might well need over the next few days. The houses of Bhuban are so close together that their thatched roofs join over the narrow alleys, cutting out the light, and only single-line pedestrian traffic is possible. None the less, in the maze of shops selling brass and metal objects for which Bhuban has a reputation, we located the bomb-seller.

The bombs were hard and round, about the size of golf balls, and were wrapped in brightly coloured paper. When thrown against something hard they exploded like army thunderflashes. These ethnic grenades scared the hell out of me, and it was hoped that they would have the same effect on a wild animal.

By the time we returned to camp Tara was fully loaded. Unhappy about this sudden extra weight, she kept whipping her trunk back, trying to undo Bhim's knots. From the front she looked like an old bag lady. Pots, pans, kerosene stoves and old sacks filled with tinned food hung from one side. Over the other flank dangled tents, sleeping bags, pillows, axes and cameras. All this paraphernalia had been placed in two white nylon hammocks that I had brought from England, so that from the back she resembled some grotesque model, wearing gigantic shoulder pads. As a deterrent against the hot sun, the top of her head had been oiled and it gleamed like a patent-leather shoe. When Gokul, eager to see her reaction, exploded a bomb beneath her feet, she displayed the same patience as a nanny with a small naughty child, simply turning her head and giving him a look as if to say, 'Silly child,' and continued trying to undo the knots. It was not surprising that she didn't react. Rajpath must have taken her through so many town festivals that she was now indifferent to ordeal by firecracker.

There are four ways to climb on to an elephant. The first, and the one that we were about to adopt, is the easiest for the passenger and the most uncomfortable for the elephant. With a command of '*Baitho!*' the elephant kneels and one clambers up on to the howdah by way of stepping on to the top of the front part of either leg, grabbing on to the ear and hauling oneself up. In the old days a ladder would be produced or one would mount from a special block. The second way is harder. Upon the command of '*Uhta! Utha!*' the elephant lifts either of its front legs and, grabbing the ear, one steps on to the leg and is raised up like an elevator. The third is over the backside. The elephant lowers one of its back legs, and one simply catches on to her tail or the crupper rope. The fourth, the expert's way, and the way that I hoped one day to achieve, is by the trunk. It looks so casual, elegant and simple. The trunk is lowered to the ground; placing a foot about in the centre, one holds both ears and is hoisted up and over.

Having awkwardly, but successfully, climbed aboard, I settled into the howdah and noticed Aditya about to mount with his boots on.

'Take off your boots,' I said.

'What?' he exclaimed crossly. 'Why?'

'I don't know why. But from now on, no boots when riding Tara.' For some inexplicable reason I felt her to be as sacred as the deck of a yacht and I was delighted when I saw Bhim nod his approval. Grumbling, Aditya untied his boots, threw them up to me and climbed aboard. Tara immediately rose to her feet and we were lifted gently upwards. Elephant-back at last, I thought happily. We really have started the journey.

An Angry Tusker

I do not know why it is, but the instant I am on
an elephant I do not feel afraid for myself or anybody else. When the
tall grass shakes and the elephants begin to scream, I ask whether it is a
tiger or a rhinoceros in exactly the same tone I should ask the servants
whether it is a partridge or a pheasant.

FANNY EDEN, *Indian Journals* 1837–1838,
Tigers, Durbars and Kings

From the very moment that Tara took her first step forward, I was
filled with a complete sense of security, cocooned, wrapped in
cotton-wool. I knew that while this wonderful, benign animal lum-
bered below me, nothing could go wrong. From twelve feet up the
view was spectacular. The landscape took on a different perspective
and one could see both far and near – the blazing yellow of a distant
mustard field or the early morning goings on over a mud wall of a
village. But it was the feeling of invincibility that struck me most. My
imagination ran riot, and I became the 'King of Bliss' surrounded by
a thousand elephants, revelling in the horror and fear of my foes.

The experts told me that it would be uncomfortable, tedious
and even painful to travel in a howdah. How wrong they were. I
found the soft swaying motion relaxing, almost too relaxing. On
occasion, I fell asleep, and just caught myself before I slid off. To
prevent this, I fashioned a sling from a length of rope and found
I could lie back with my feet hanging over her backside. Then,

after plugging in my Walkman, I could recline like a maharaja, listening to the strains of Italian opera while a huge, never-changing, empty sky passed by overhead. Occasionally, like a tiny silver arrow, an aeroplane would flash far above. I felt sorry for the passengers squeezed into their pressurized chamber, hurrying from one destination to the next, unable to see the beauty that I was so fortunate to be enjoying. Gradually I was slowing down, slowing down to the pace of a country in which if one moves fast, one misses everything – and like a patient tutor Tara was influencing me, showing me the way.

We were now climbing steadily and passing through Orissa's mining belt – a dull, wide, angry landscape, dotted with huge rocky escarpments gouged out and scarred by blasting and bulldozers. In the distance I could see the forested ranges of Daitari shimmering blue in the heat haze. It was hot. As elephants do not sweat, Tara cooled herself down by looping her trunk into her mouth, extracting a mixture of spit and water and blowing it in a fine spray over her flanks and under her belly. Elephants, like camels, can store water. They have a kind of shut-off valve system that they can open and close as they wish. As the sun became fiercer, she piled a bonnet of straw and leaves on top of her head. Her great ears, the smooth skin behind their wide spread knotted with thick veins, flapped rhythmically, acting as ventilation under which Bhim would occasionally stretch out his legs and manipulate her with his toes to urge her on. Each toe had a life of its own, pushing, probing and playing like the fingers of a concert pianist. Then he would sit back on the front of the howdah and work her head with the heels of his feet, pushing forward and down. No commands were necessary. It was all being done by touch. Bhim told me to watch his movements carefully and learn. A true master remains silent. Considering my appalling Hindi accent, this would certainly make life easier.

Another example of Bhim's expertise came when Gokul, who would be walking alongside us, would change into the driving seat. Tara's pace would then alter considerably and she would slow right down, however much Gokul shrieked commands at her. She knew instinctively that she was now in control and exploited the situation mercilessly.

We made camp under a lone peepul tree on top of a small hillock by the side of the road. The heat had sapped our strength and we slept for most of the afternoon. In the evening I went to feed Tara her *gur*. She greeted me with an affectionate rumble, wrapped her trunk around me, drawing me closer, searching my body for her treat. The vet at Nandankanan had also given me some deworming powder for her, a little of which I had hidden in a thick ball of *gur*.

'*Lay, lay*, Tara!' I commanded.

She opened her mouth wide, exposing tiny six-inch tusks on either side and I caught a glimpse of her gigantic molars. I placed the ball on her fat, pink tongue, which was as soft as a blancmange, and watched the obvious pleasure appear on her face. It changed quickly to one of 'You can't fool me' as she delicately removed the ball, placed it on the ground, broke it open with her trunk, blew the powder out, remoulded it and popped it back into her mouth. She did, however, like some medicines. As I kissed her goodnight, she reached into the top pocket of my shirt and pulled out a new packet of Setlers which she swallowed whole with relish.

Over the next few days we crossed heavily wooded highlands, which in some places were as high as three and a half thousand feet, to Keonjhar, the capital of this large hilly district. The rocky ground, called laterite or iron sandstone, was of a sombre, dark-reddish colour. When I picked up a stone I was surprised by its lightness and the large, round holes, like those of a sponge. All ancient temples, forts and palaces in Orissa are built with this stone, and, mixed with gravel, so are most of the roads. Our progress was slow, as Tara picked her way carefully, avoiding the sharp stones to prevent injuring her sensitive feet.

As we reached the summits which, from below, appeared as sharp peaks, we crossed extensive tablelands filled with green paddy in which women, wearing a colourful blaze of saris and large cane cone-shaped hats, were reaping the harvest. As the sun reached its zenith they shaded themselves under the trees, singing and combing each other's hair in the heat. We heard them giggling as we passed and they waved shyly.

'It reminds me of summer in England,' Aditya remarked.

'I didn't know you'd been there,' I said.

'Yes, in 1970. I worked in Kent, picking hops, although I didn't sit around like these girls. I worked from 5.30 in the morning until seven o'clock at night. He was a bastard, that foreman, a real driver of slaves.'

'That's probably exactly what he thought you were,' I joked, 'fresh off a boat that had sneaked in somewhere on the coast at night.'

'I most certainly was not,' he replied indignantly. 'I hitchhiked all the way from India. But, let me tell you, I felt like one the way that I was treated. I don't have many good memories of England at that time.'

'Well,' I murmured philosophically, 'here we are now, riding across India together on an elephant. What could be more apt?'

At that moment Tara shot out her trunk and grabbed a pile of paddy that was laid out to dry on the roadside. Bhim picked up the *ankush* and jabbed the sharp spiked end into the top of her head. She squealed, violently shaking her head in pain. I watched with fascinated horror as a large drop of blood bubbled from her skin. With a roar of rage I tore the *ankush* from Bhim's hand, grabbed hold of one of the ropes and swung on to the ground.

'That's it!' I yelled. 'The journey's over. I will not have my elephant hurt. You can all find your own way back.'

I stamped off down the road. Ten minutes later Aditya caught up with me. I stared at the bloody tip of the *ankush*.

'Forget it, Aditya,' I said. 'You can't say anything . . .'

'Now listen!' Aditya shouted. 'Who in hell do you think you are? Elephant Bill? What do you know about elephants? Bhim would not use the *ankush* unless it was absolutely necessary. Before you interrupt, let me tell you what he told me. Tara was stealing. And I have just had to pay that poor farmer compensation. It is not Tara's fault, though. She was taught these tricks by Rajpath. Many mendicants literally hold people to ransom by getting their elephants to pick up the paddy, unless the farmers pay up. Bhim has to break Tara of the habit of stealing and the *ankush* is the only way to make her understand.'

I sat down and stared moodily at my bare feet.

'Come on, Mark. Elephants are big, powerful creatures. If you start pampering them, you are in trouble. They are intelligent, cunning and deceitful. Believe me, the old man knows what he's doing. If he fails to convert her now, she will only get worse.'

'All right, I'm sorry,' I said, slightly mollified. 'I guess I have a lot to learn, but one thing is for sure, you won't find me doing that. Shameless bribery with *gur* rather than sharp jabs with the *ankush* is going to be my method.'

'We'll see,' he replied. 'Just wait until you start riding her.'

We walked back to Tara who did not seem at all affected by her punishment. She was pulling up roots, smacking them against her legs to remove the earth, then stuffing them into her mouth. We climbed back on board and Bhim pointed at her head. 'See, Raja-sahib. I fix.' A small poultice of herbs was attached to the wound. 'No hurt now. Bhim sorry, but Raja-sahib must learn. Mummy learning also.'

Apart from the numerous anti-elephant *machans* dotted every-where, the paddy fields that we now passed were surrounded by anti-elephant ditches seven feet deep, five feet wide at the top, tapering to about two feet at the bottom. Wild elephants are power-less to cross them except during the monsoons when the ditches silt up. Around the planted fields there were fences of twisted creepers in which wild mint grew in abundance, filling the air with its sharp aroma.

Then we entered the silent darkness of the forest and all was still again. Tara suddenly stopped, her huge ears spreading out-wards. She extended her trunk upwards and moved it from side to side scanning and smelling the air.

'*Haathi*,' Bhim whispered. 'Close.'

Aditya reached for his camera bag. In the process he knocked it against a metal strut. With a sharp downward gesture of his hand Bhim indicated to him to keep still and with another instructed Gokul to climb aboard. There was no noise, only the sound of dripping water. Then a sharp 'Tuk, tuk, tuk' split the silence and a coppersmith bird rang its alarm bell.

From the corner of my eye I caught a slight movement. A soft sound, almost inaudible, was the only indication that the foliage was being gently brushed aside. Like ghosts, three female elephants appeared and stood motionless on the road in front of us. I could feel Tara trembling beneath me. The wild elephants let out a deep rumble and extended their trunks towards Tara. They seemed much larger than her, more muscular, their bodies sculpted like sheet armour on a tank. Then as quickly and quietly as they had appeared, they disappeared.

I let out my breath and was about to reach for a cigarette when Bhim gave another of his urgent hand signals. We heard a movement, as if the grass were being crushed by some huge, unidentified force, and suddenly a large male elephant with tusks almost three foot long confronted us. The tusks were not white, as I had expected, but yellow, and the tips dark from where he had been digging in the earth. Tara was trembling violently and Bhim was having trouble holding her steady. We were so close I could see the flies clustered around the tusker's mean little eyes. Without warning he rapped his trunk on the ground, emitting a terrifying sound that somebody once described as like 'shaking a large sheet of thin metal' caused by air being driven out of the trunk as it strikes the ground.

'Quick,' Bhim hissed. 'He angry. Throw bombs.'

Gokul, who always carried a permanent supply, like a kid with fireworks, hurled one on to the ground. Nothing happened. It failed to explode. The tusker took one step forward, throwing his trunk contemptuously into the air, emitting a terrible shrill trumpet, as if warning us to keep our distance. It was so loud, so enveloping that one's senses reeled. I shook my head to clear it.

'For Christ's sake,' I whispered in desperation. 'Throw another.'

Leaving nothing to chance, Bhim picked up a bomb, laid it on the flat of the howdah and hit it with the *ankush*. There was a blinding flash, a puff of blue smoke, and when it had cleared the road was empty. We could hear the elephants crashing away through the trees, as delayed shock set in. But in that moment of silence, before terror turns to laughter, the primal energy of the absent beast still vibrated in the void. It seemed almost impossible to go forward. The silence of the jungle was no longer tranquil. It had become predatory.

'What would have happened if we hadn't got the bombs?' I asked shaken.

'Maybe trouble,' Bhim laughed. 'Forget tell you. Mummy on heat.' He pointed to the temporal glands, two small holes from which a black viscous fluid was oozing, on either side of her face.

I remembered my amazement when I had seen an elephant's erect penis at the zoo. It was at least four foot long and as thick as a man's leg.

Tara's Tantrum

By the time we reached the outskirts of Keonjhar it was dark and I was both hoarse from shouting commands and exhausted. Once an old British hill station, the town lay at some elevation and for the last ten miles I had forced Tara up steep inclines. After that the thought of spending the night under canvas was just too hideous to contemplate. I went to visit the Collector, a charming, easy-going man, who immediately arranged for us to sleep in the Circuit House, built by a former Maharaja of Keonjhar some eighty years ago, which was now usually reserved for visiting dignitaries and judges.

It was a splendid, solid example of English Colonial-cum-Indian palace architecture, spoilt only by a coat of vile mauve paint. We had the place to ourselves. After chaining Tara to a mango tree in the large, walled garden, we spread ourselves out in a suite of four rooms on the first floor leading on to a spacious veranda. It was surrounded by a pretty wrought-iron balcony, furnished with old-fashioned teak and wicker planters' chairs with extending leg-rests, marble-topped ebony tables and, best of all, a large refrigerator which we quickly stocked with beer. As we sat looking out over the twinkling lights of Keonjhar, a white-coated attendant filled our glasses and looked disdainfully at Indrajit's line of dripping clothes festooned around the balcony like mourning flags. Obviously he had been used to more respectable guests.

After the luxury of hot baths and a decent dinner, Aditya and I lay out in the long chairs in the darkness.

'We might spend a few days here,' he remarked, settling himself more comfortably and taking a long pull of beer. 'We're well on schedule and it would do us all good to take a rest,' he added, noticing me trying to sit sideways in the chair.

'No, I'm fine,' I winced. 'I think we should push on.'

'As you wish. But I was really thinking of Tara. Bhim has told me she is a little under the weather.'

'What?' I said, falling into his carefully laid trap. 'In that case, we must rest.'

Like Tara, with her *gur*, Aditya had successfully discovered my Achilles heel. Unable to walk, I crawled over to the side of the balcony. I could just make her out, dusting herself happily while leaning up against the tree, with one back leg crossed over the other.

'Goodnight, my love,' I shouted. She turned, lifting her trunk, emitting a half trumpet, half squeak, like a suppressed sneeze. I smiled happily. I was getting there.

In the morning Aditya and I set out in a rickshaw to visit the old palace of Keonjhar which we had been told was just a crumbling empty shell. The rickshaw driver's leg muscles bulged with the effort and his breath came in short, sharp bursts as we climbed steadily out of town. Then we picked up speed, freewheeling down hills lined with shops where men made metal pots, banging them into shape with small hammers. Out of the clouds appeared a fine crenellated wall, overgrown with creepers and furnished with tactically sited look-out turrets embellished with arrow slits. Leaving the rickshaw we passed through an ancient gateway, its great wooden doors hanging askew from rotten hinges. We could make out the ruined palace overgrown with jungle and stained green with mildew, but still showing traces of former elegance. We wandered down a weed-covered pathway, choked with wild roses and shaded by towering palm trees.

At the main entrance, guarded by a pair of heavy bronze cannons moulded in the shape of tigers, we were met by a group of scruffy young urchins who announced that they were the keepers of the palace and would be pleased to show us around. They led us into the Durbar Hall, which had been capped at one time by a fine frescoed rotunda and was now open to the sky. The floor was covered in bird shit. Graffiti were scrawled on the walls. 'The world is a servant to money' and 'Life is nothing but pain.' In the ballroom, they told us, a vast crystal chandelier used to hang from the ceiling, where a family of swallows now had their nest. As we felt our way along dark, dripping corridors, bats erupted around us and screeched away, brushing our faces with their velvet wings. In the Deity room a black outline was all that was left of a solid gold statue, stolen twenty years ago, and in a corner, flaking with rust, was the Royal Nagara – a huge metal war drum. Noting my interest, one of the little boys explained with the air of a professional guide that there were once two war drums covered in human skin. In warning against invading armies, they would reverberate of their own accord.

'What happened to the other one?' I asked.

'Gone walking, sir. To lake.'

Under a large mango tree, which we were told was a thousand years old, stone slabs covered a dried-up spring. Legend said that anybody entering the water disappeared. Keonjhar took its name from this. It means 'spring' in Oriya.

Our young guides ushered us into a large, pretty courtyard surrounded by small pavilions. In the centre stood a marble fountain designed as the open petals of a lotus flower. The floors of the pavilions had once been mosaic and were still studded with a few remaining pieces of lapis lazuli. An ornate, gilded, empty frame was propped up against a wall, a reminder of an opulence long gone. This was the entertainment chamber where once the Maharaja had received his visitors, plying them with opium-based sherbets and sweetmeats as they relaxed on silk bolsters, while dancing girls had whirled in front of them. To make his foreign guests feel at home, the ruler had commissioned carved scenes, which still ran along one wall – a two-masted ship in full sail; a lady in European costume with a small boy in knickerbockers hanging on to her full skirts; a train puffing over a bridge. One of the boys asked as we were leaving if we wished to meet Her Highness the Rajmata.

'The Rajmata!' Aditya exclaimed incredulously. 'She still lives here?'

We waited in a small, dripping courtyard surrounded by tubs of long, cactus-like plants called 'mother-in-law's tongues' and from whose shape and sharpness they have taken their name. Where once we would have been forbidden to enter we now stood – in the old *zenana*.

The boys reappeared carrying in their arms an old lady dressed in a simple cotton sari and scuffed rubber sandals. After laying out a strip of torn Aubusson carpet, they placed her carefully in a rickety wicker chair. Behind her, in the gloom, her attendants fluttered about like ghostly moths, their faces veiled. The boys informed us that the Rajmata was unable to speak, but she could hear and see.

Aditya stepped forward and touched her feet in obeisance. For a moment the sad eyes cleared and she smiled gently, as if remembering better times; times when the palace had bustled with activity, times of glittering banquets, the rustle of silken saris, of colour and, above all, of respect. Now she was reduced to this, a proud old woman left with nothing. A wave of great sadness swept over me.

The boys' devotion to the old lady was touching. No one looked after her now, they told us angrily as we were leaving. Her relations had abandoned her. She had been robbed at gunpoint three times. Everything had been taken. They had begged her not to keep her valuables under her bed, but, like many old women, she did not trust banks.

'You know these western states were once famous for human sacrifice,' Aditya told me on the way back in the rickshaw. 'Traditionally, the Rajas of this state had the right during their coronations to have a man brought in front of them, whereupon they would cut off his head, and give rent-free land to his family as compensation. After the British arrived and banned capital punishment, the Commissioner, on hearing of this custom, quickly travelled to Keonjhar to put a stop to it. As you can imagine, everybody was highly upset, but the Commissioner, a practical fellow, managed to appease the ruling Raja and solve the problem. The chosen man was duly brought forward. The Raja swung at him with his sword without actually making contact and the victim collapsed on the ground feigning death. He was then ordered to disappear from the kingdom and to be very careful never to be seen by the Raja. He was in fact declared dead and the family duly compensated.'

24

'Typical British ingenuity,' I crowed. 'At least we did achieve something.'

Early next morning, Aditya and I were woken by a frantic Indrajit and Gokul. 'Tara escape!' they exclaimed, 'in big tank [reservoir]. Won't come out.'

'Where's Bhim?' I growled, sleepily.

'Sleeping. Drink too much rum last night, so we take her for bath.'

'Wake him up now and meet us at the tank.'

When we arrived there was no sign of Tara. The surface of the water was calm. Alarmingly, the tank was enormous. (I remembered the case of an elephant that went for a two-hundred-mile swim, island-hopping across the Bay of Bengal. It took twelve years to complete its journey and the distance between some of the islands was at least a mile.) Suddenly from the far side of the tank, the tip of Tara's trunk broke the surface, blowing a spray of water like a fountain into the air. With a trumpet of pleasure she flung herself forward like a porpoise and disappeared again, delighting the large crowd which had by now gathered around the tank.

Bhim arrived carrying a spear, the *ankush*, a selection of fruit and a large sack of *gur*. 'Not Mummy's fault,' he said angrily. 'Gokul forget chain legs. Rajpath warn.'

Gokul squeaked with indignation stating that he was unaware of Tara's penchant and if Bhim had not drunk so much, this never would have happened. Aditya calmed them down before a fight broke out, suggesting they should concentrate their energies on getting her out.

Standing in the shallows, Bhim started calling Tara, a banana   25 in his outstretched hand. She immediately reacted, came surging across the tank to stop a few yards from the bank. In the meantime, as Gokul could not swim, Indrajit, armed with the spear, had managed to circle behind her. He waited, treading water frantically with the tip of the spear aimed at her backside. As she came a little closer and reached out her trunk, Bhim retreated, enticingly. She came closer still, almost into the shallows. With a quick lunge, she whipped the banana out of his hand, popped it into her mouth and reversed into the water. Turning to face Indrajit, who had been almost swamped by the wave, she blew a jet of water at him, performed a kind of elephant back-flip and surged away, trumpeting triumphantly. The audience applauded deliriously.

This ploy was repeated a number of times. All were unsuccessful. Finally Bhim turned to me. 'Raja-sahib call Mummy.'

Aditya had gone to call the police to see if they could disperse the crowd that was not helping matters. He returned with one policeman who, upon seeing Tara cavorting in the water, tucked his bamboo cane under his arm and settled down to enjoy the fun.

I followed Bhim's instructions. 'Tara! Tara!' I yelled authoritatively, waving a lump of *gur* in my hand. '*A dhur! A dhur! Lay! Lay!*' The people watching howled with laughter on hearing my accent. Some of them mimicked me accurately.

Again Tara came quickly across the lake. At the sight of the *gur*, she placed two large front feet on the muddy bank. I gave her a small piece and then, as quickly as possible, grabbed hold of one of her ears to try swinging up on her back. She turned quickly. For a moment I was pulled through the water like a beginner trying to water ski, letting go as I swallowed a mouthful of dirty water. I started to swim back, gasping and choking. I felt something long and sinuous encircle me, and, like a lifesaver rescuing a drowning man, Tara pushed me forward, depositing me in a wet bundle in the shallows. She trumpeted again and looked at me mischievously before returning to her watery playground. 'Mummy no come now,' Bhim stated. 'We leave her. Mummy come out when cold.'

That evening, almost twelve hours later, I was sitting on the veranda of the Circuit House when Gokul shouted excitedly, 'Tara coming!' Looking down, I saw her trotting happily into the garden. At last, I thought, thank God for that. Unfortunately our troubles were not over. Each time Bhim and Gokul tried to shackle her, she backed away, after ripping the chains from Bhim's hands and throwing them into the air.

We tried the old food trick. One of us fed her while the other tried to snap the two front chains together. It failed. After shutting the garden gate, we drove her into a small area surrounded by two walls. We advanced on her purposefully, shouting, '*Baitho, baitho!*' and jabbing the spear into her back legs. She charged at one of the walls, almost demolishing it. Slightly stunned, Tara stood quietly for a moment. Seizing his chance, Bhim quickly scrambled on to her and took control with the *ankush*. Gokul then chained her. She looked unusually remorseful, squeezing her eyes shut when I rapped the end of her trunk with a small stick.

Tara's tantrum was over, but I couldn't be angry for long. After all, it was Sunday and Gandhi's birthday. It was a holiday and she deserved some fun.

Death in the Jungle

We headed north-west into the state of Mayurbhanj, traversing a high plateau towards the great tiger sanctuary of the Simlipals. To our left, a few miles from the Bihar border where it looped down to its most southerly point, lay the ancient city of Kitching, in the tenth and eleventh centuries AD the capital of the Bhanja kings.

Having waited so long to ride Tara, I now dreaded it, the pain was so great. To ease the stiffness in my joints, I walked. We passed a procession of men carrying a small bundle wrapped in straw and strung from a long pole. A police chief idled slowly in a jeep behind. We stopped to talk with him. The bundle contained the body of a young tribal girl who had been found early that morning raped and mutilated by the roadside. Tara became increasingly fidgety, as if the sight and the smell of this morbid situation was utterly distasteful to her.

Curious, I asked Bhim whether he had ever known an elephant to have eaten flesh. He shook his head vehemently, then narrowed his eyes as if searching for something that had happened a long time ago. Reluctantly, he recalled an incident. It had happened during a state occasion. A maharaja was being carried in a silver howdah on the back of a ceremonial elephant, ridden by its mahout. Suddenly the elephant snaked its trunk back grabbing the mahout's leg and pulling him to the ground. As in the old days, when in certain states in India executions were carried out, the elephant stomped on the mahout's head, splitting it like a ripe melon. Gath-

28

ering the gory contents in its trunk, it had blown out a bloody spray, spattering the Maharaja. Shocked and outraged, the Maharaja immediately ordered the elephant to be destroyed. The other mahouts, however, begged him to reconsider. This mahout, they told him, had for many years treated the elephant with the utmost cruelty. The Maharaja, passionately fond of this favourite elephant, believed their stories and spared it. The elephant never misbehaved again.

'There was one situation in which an elephant did actually eat a human being,' I told him. 'It happened in a zoo in Switzerland many years ago.' Bhim looked at me with disbelief. 'This elephant called Chang was punished for misbehaving and confined to his stable. Chang had a great admirer, a young girl who was so upset that she broke into the zoo overnight to feed and console him. She did not return home. In the morning the elephant keepers found traces of blood on the floor and, lying amongst the fodder, a human hand and a toe. On further investigation Chang's droppings revealed her undigested clothes, hat and handbag. The keeper persuaded the authorities to spare the elephant's life, but some years later Chang grabbed his keeper and battered him to death against the bars. Chang was then destroyed.'

'Pah!' Bhim uttered contemptuously, spitting out a thin red stream of betel juice, and, leaning forward, covered Tara's great ears. 'No listen Raja-sahib, Mummy. He telling bad things.'

About eight miles from Joshipur, the point of entry into the Simlipals, I got on Tara and we joined a busy trunk road which straddles the continent from Calcutta to Bombay. The harder I was on her, the better she behaved and Bhim told me that I was beginning to make progress. My main problem, however, was   29 avoiding the trucks that thundered by perilously close. I spent a tiring day digging my big toe under her right ear and shouting, '*Chi, chi*,' to turn her on to the verge. Once there, progress was even slower. It was lined with trees. At every one she helped herself to the overhanging branches, ripping them off and plucking the leaves, then stripping the bark before moving on to the next. Determined to put a stop to this greed, I banged the blunt end of the *ankush* repeatedly on her head. She simply shook her head and took no notice, occasionally showing her mild displeasure by blasting me in a fine spray of spittle.

She was none the less beginning to earn her keep. A number of the trucks that passed us would stop. The co-driver would stretch out a hand and place a coin in the tip of her trunk which she would then curl upwards and deposit the money on her head. Blessed by Ganesh for a safe journey, the drivers would clasp their hands together, make their *namastes* and move on. Sometimes her trunk would shoot through the open window, almost demanding payment. When we reached Singada, our pockets jingled with coins. We now had established a way of financing our journey. Rajpath had taught her well.

A large weekly market was taking place at Singada. I threaded Tara through the mass of humanity and animals, causing a stampede. Bullocks and goats knocked over food stalls and Tara liberally helped herself to the spoils. Soon our jingling pockets were empty as we forked out compensation. Squatting in small groups, tribal women radiant in brilliant red and blue saris were selling *handia*, the local hooch, handing it out in coconut shells. Anklets jingling, others weaved through the crowds replenishing supplies, their smooth, strong, braceleted arms supporting large terracotta gourds on their heads. Everyone appeared to be drunk, throwing around their hard-earned money liberally, enticed by the miracles that were on offer.

Two travelling Rajput medicine doctors, wearing bright-red turbans over strong, thin, aquiline faces, excitedly advertised the virtues of their wares which lay coated with flies in small trays in front of them. Most popular were the aphrodisiacs – dried intestines of snakes, toads' feet and a particularly strong brew of cobra tongues and boars' semen. At another stall a large crowd gathered round a man surrounded by baskets containing many different kinds of snake. The crowd gasped as he rolled up his sleeves. Taking a snake's head, he forced its mouth open and plunged the fangs into his arm. Writhing in mock agony, he tied a bright-red thread just above where the snake had struck, and then slowly straightened his arm. Miraculously he was cured. The threads, he extolled to the crowd, were blessed and stopped the effects of the poison instantly. He was a good salesman and business was brisk.

Short of Joshipur we stopped at a roadside tea-house. A dazzling array of trucks was parked outside. A small wiry man with slanting eyes, his face a deep ruddy colour, engaged me in conversation. He was Nepalese and a co-driver on one of the trucks.

'Take me with you to England,' he pleaded. 'I will be your bodyguard. I am excellent at fighting.' He pulled up his shirt exposing a livid lumpy scar that ran from his navel to his right nipple. 'I killed the man who gave me this,' he said proudly. 'These people,' he continued contemptuously, gesturing at some tough-looking characters who were sitting drinking tea, 'are weak. Nobody can match a Gurkha.'

'I don't need a bodyguard,' I replied. 'You see I have an elephant.'

'Ah, in that case you are in good company. It is not my lucky day.'

As we entered Joshipur, a motorcyclist wearing a uniform, goggles and a leather aviator's cap, slowed down, gave us a curious look and then drove on. He then stopped, turned round and passed us again. He repeated this manoeuvre several times, as if unsure of something. Finally he shouted, 'Are you *Haathi* from Konarak?'

'No!' Aditya yelled back. 'We are the *Haathi* from Calcutta. The *Haathi* from Konarak be arriving later.'

'More *Haathis* arriving?' he said puzzled.

'Yes,' Aditya said airily. 'Tomorrow one from Delhi and then another from Bombay.'

'Oh, goodness me, this is most confusing,' and the man raced off.

'Bloody officials,' Aditya laughed, 'that's fixed him.'

Joshipur is where one actually enters the park, but it is from Baripada, the capital of the state of Mayurbhanj, some forty miles away, that the permissions are granted. Through the window in the office I noticed a powerful radio.

'Would it be possible to send a message to Baripada?' I asked politely of a young bespectacled forest officer.

'It is not working,' he snapped nervously. 'Park closed. No one allowed in.'

'But your brochure,' I argued, 'informs one that the park opens on the first of October. It is now the fifth.' There was no answer. Two mystified Australians, who had come all the way from Delhi, were still waiting after four days to see the game park.

'We are wasting our time, Mark,' Aditya said. 'Indrajit should drive us to Baripada and we will find the man in charge. Maybe we can contact the Maharaja for whom you have a letter. He might be able to help. In the meantime, Bhim, Gokul and Khusto can stay with Tara.'

When we reached Baripada we discovered that the Maharaja was 'out of station' and the forest officer had disappeared, 'gone to the market', we were told. Through local information we found out the reason. There was a man-eating tiger abroad and it had just killed somebody in the south of the park. No one was allowed in. Desperate that we should cross this great game park, whose beauty had been extolled to me from the beginning of my journey through Orissa, I telephoned the authorities in Bhubaneshwar. I pleaded and pushed. The park was enormous, I argued. Over three thousand square kilometres. It was unlikely that I would bump into the tiger. Finally, we were granted full permission to go anywhere in the park, but only by jeep, not with the elephant. Reluctantly I agreed. It was better than nothing but I felt sad that I wouldn't be able to share this wilderness with Tara.

We waited three hours for the forest officer, a tall man with a limp handshake, who seemed anxious to be rid of us, issuing a letter immediately and nervously avoiding any reference to the man-eater. On the way back to Joshipur we stopped to stretch our legs at a roadside tribal shrine. Effigies of cows and horses and two black granite elephants stood garlanded by night jasmine. An old *pandit* came out of the shrine and blessed us. In the darkness Aditya and I looked at one another.

'Are you thinking what I'm thinking?' he said.

'Yes,' I replied.

We opened the letter and studied it under the jeep's headlights. It was addressed to the officer in charge at Joshipur.

I talked with CWLW at ten p.m. today and he confirmed our earlier decision re the pet elephant will not be allowed inside Simlipal. They may keep the elephant at Joshipur. Accompany these persons in park jeep to Chahala and Barehipani but avoid Jenabil because of the man-eating problem. But do not tell them this. The roads are not OK. Tell that.

'But the people who collect honey from those sheer rock faces are deeper in the park. We'll miss seeing them,' I said. We had been told about them in Bhubaneshwar. Their methods of collecting honey were spectacular and unique to the Simlipals.

Indrajit came over and Aditya translated the contents of the letter. He was silent for a moment. 'Perhaps we lose park jeep in jungle,' he shrugged. 'If lost, must go where we can.'

The next morning Indrajit, Aditya and myself left the camp. Earlier I had asked Bhim if he would like to come, but he wanted to stay with Tara. 'Mummy unhappy both Raja-sahib and Bhim go away three days,' he said. 'One day okay.'

The park jeep escorted us into the Simlipals. It was like entering another world; a world that had been untouched for centuries. The tracks were overgrown, lined by tall sal trees. The air was fresh after the monsoons. In sunny clearings peacocks stood motionless, fanning out their glorious feathers, and high above them mynah birds chattered noisily. At intervals we would catch the flash of gold and white and a spotted deer would turn to look at us before picking its feet daintily through the undergrowth. Everywhere was the evidence of elephants, old and fresh droppings littered the

34

road. In the 1986 census four hundred and fifty elephants had been counted and as many as ninety tigers.

Through a bower of orchid-lined trees, we arrived at Chahala, an old shooting lodge of the Maharaja of Mayurbhanj, now converted into a tourist camp. It was gothic in design with vaulted ceilings and large open fireplaces. It had been painted a hideous violet and green. Surrounding it was a deep anti-elephant trench and, beyond, strategically placed salt-licks for game. At five o'clock the next morning, as the mist still hung heavy in the air, we watched bison and barking deer approach the salt-licks, followed by a small herd of elephants, including two babies, who held their mothers' tails with tiny trunks. From the distance came the deep cough of a tiger. The animals moved away quickly, the little elephants squealing in alarm.

From a raised log cabin at Barehipani, the source of the Buldhabalanga River, we gazed across a wide gorge and watched a thirteen-hundred-foot waterfall thunder beneath us. In Hindi *barehi* means 'thread' and *pani* 'water'. In the dry season, only a thread of water falls like a single silver arrow. The old forest ranger complained bitterly about the elephants. Every week, he told us, they destroyed his garden. Most years the log cabin had to be rebuilt because wild elephants rubbed their sides against the thick wooden poles. I thought sadly of Tara. How she would have loved this paradise where elephants roamed free, untouched and undisturbed.

As there was no news of the man-eater, our guides thought it safe to take us to Nawana, the village of the honey collectors. We descended from the hills crossing wide grassy meadows, alive with wild flowers. On the outskirts of the village, we parked the jeeps and entered a small mud-walled courtyard. It was empty except for a young man with one leg. The villagers, he told us, were far away on the other side of the park taking honey from the tree bees. It was only during the winter that they collected from the rock bees. I was bitterly disappointed.

'How is the honey collected?' Aditya asked him in Hindi.

'It is a dangerous business, sir. We lower ourselves on thick vines down the rock faces in which the bees make their nests in small caves. When we find a nest we light a torch and throw it in. The bees come swarming out and we collect the honey.'

'Don't you get stung?'

'Sometimes, sir. But we smear our bodies with herbs and always chant our mantras before work. On a good day we can collect twenty-five kilos of honey.'

'What happened to your leg?' Aditya asked, I thought rather impolitely.

He smiled ruefully and rubbed the stump. 'It is our wives, sir. They tie the vines on to trees at the top of the rock face. There they stand guard. Unfortunately,' he added, 'my wife liked another man. It was a long fall. I was lucky.'

I told the park rangers that I wanted to talk with the villagers when they returned from collecting honey. They agreed to let us stay at Nawana. They would return in a few hours to collect us.

'You want to go Jenabil? Now chance,' Indrajit said excitedly after they had left. 'Maybe seeing tiger?' Aditya and I looked at each other nervously.

'Well, why not?' I said to Aditya after some deliberation. 'We've missed the rock bees and we've come all this way. Let's go.'

The track was overgrown and from the absence of tyre marks nothing had passed this way for months. A tree blocked our way. Struggling to lift it we disturbed a herd of wild elephants feeding near by, camouflaged by the solid green wall of the jungle. The ground shook as they crashed away, trumpeting wildly. At Jenabil the tourist lodge was empty. In the small village Indrajit found a man who knew where the tiger had killed. At first he was reluctant to take us, but with the promise of a healthy reward, he agreed. I told Indrajit to ask him whether we might catch a glimpse of the tiger. The man looked astounded and launched into an urgent tirade.

'This is not a joke, sir,' he replied angrily. 'This is a big, male tiger. It was a man-eater that killed my friend, and it will kill again.' Our bravado deserted us instantly. We fell silent. The man continued. 'We are poor people, sir. We go into the forest to collect *lac* [resin produced by coccid insects from which incense is made] from the trees. Each day, before entering the forest, our *pandit* tells us which side of the road to go to avoid *bagh*. That day there were ten of us. The *pandit* told us to go to the right but my friend, Sri Ram Naik, decided he would go the other way. A few days earlier he had spotted a good healthy tree. He was a brave man and had, on several occasions, fended off *bagh* with his axe. It is an everyday occurrence. We and *bagh* must try and live together. He was big man, like you,' he pointed at me. 'He took his young son with him. His remains are still there. The police were too frightened to go in to collect them. We must be very careful, *bagh* is still around.'

We reached a place where an axe cut marked a tree standing by the road. 'This is the place,' he said quietly. 'We go in here. Take sticks and make plenty of noise for *bagh* can be sitting two feet away and you will not see him.'

Aditya and I realized we were embarking on something both dangerous and stupid. We had no guns, only elephant bombs, which Indrajit cheerfully distributed to each of us. He seemed oblivious of the danger.

We stepped cautiously into the jungle, up to our waists in thick undergrowth. Large bamboo clumps, caressed by the wind, rustled urgently, warning us to take heed. We followed the guide in single file, Aditya and I firmly in the middle. Indrajit took up the rear. At intervals the guide would stop and check his route. Finding another cut in a tree, he moved on. We yelled. We shouted. We beat the bushes, feeling naked and defenceless. We reached a clearing. The bushes were flat, the surrounding trees raked with claw marks. Pointing at the dried muddy ground, the guide indicated large round indentations, the size of soup-plates – the tiger's pug marks.

On a small outcrop of rock, a faded blood smear; then a rubber sandal, and another – they were an odd pair. Close by a torn and bloody *lunghi* lay rotting in the ground. Finally a skull, gleaming yellow in the pale sun.

'It was here, sirs, that it happened,' he told us. 'My friend was looking up at this tree. *Bagh* struck silently from the back. From the other side of the road we could hear his screams. We rushed over, but he was already dead. The *bagh* had him by the throat. We tried to recover the body but *bagh* was too big and too angry. He came at us, and we ran.' Our guide shivered as he looked up at the tree. ' "O my Father I am dead." Those were his last words. His son told us.' He shivered again. 'We must hurry out of this place, sirs. It is not safe.'

I turned the skull over, disturbing a colony of ants, feeding on a flap of skin. There was nothing else. The man had been completely devoured. No bones, just the skull left as a warning. I wanted to take it but Aditya stopped me.

'Leave it,' he advised me. 'It has become part of his jungle.'

We collected the remains of his things. Now a small pathetic bundle, once worn by a strong, brave man. They deserved better than to rot in the jungle; we would take what was left to the Ganges for immersion in the holy river.

Our guide took us to the dead man's house. It was empty. His family had already left, paid a compensation of 2,000 rupees. A few broken cooking pots littered the floor. Stuck to a mud wall were coloured crayon drawings done by his children; of a field, of a cow and of a man looking up at a tree – behind him stood a yellow-striped cat with a big pink tongue and long whiskers.

If the welcome I received from Tara was an indication of her affection, I was a happy man. She positively vibrated with excitement, coiling and uncoiling her trunk like a giant watchspring, straining against her chains and uttering sneezes of contentment. For a change she did not immediately open her mouth. She simply touched my face with the wet tip of her trunk and stood perfectly still, her eyes closed, resting against me gently. A feeling of pure pleasure swept over me and then one of equal panic as in just over a month I would have to say goodbye and would probably never see her again.

Bhim wanted us to visit his family in Baripada. As we left, Tara seemed almost resentful, hurling a branch petulantly into the air. Bhim's mother and father lived in an old tiled house which stood defiantly, like an ancient spider, in an encroaching cobweb of modern buildings on the outskirts of the town. In a neat room dimly lit by oil lamps and a small cooking fire, a tall, elderly man sat erect in a rocking chair. When we entered, he came quickly to his feet belying his age, and saluted smartly. Unlike Bhim, his face was curiously unlined, almost boyish, and, apart from one rheumy eye that glittered milkily in the gloom, he seemed in the best of health. When my eyes adjusted to the darkness, I noticed his wife squatting in the corner, fussing over some pots. After offering us tea, she returned to her place, but I could feel her accusing look boring into me. She mumbled something and Bhim laughed in embarrassment.

'She worried Raja-sahib take only boy England. Never come home.'

Aditya took both her hands in his, and reassured her that this was not true. She seemed to relax a little but still continued to eye me with suspicion.

The old man was anxious to talk of the old days, and in a soft proud voice told us he had been the chief mahout of the late Maharaja and during his tenure had often been to the Sonepur Mela. There he had purchased elephants for 6,000 rupees each and had taken three months to ride them back. At one time there had been twenty elephants in the royal stables. They were so well trained that during tiger shoots they had moved so quietly not even a leaf was disturbed on the trees.

He touched the rocking chair proudly. It had been presented to him by the Maharaja when he retired. As Aditya and I were leaving, he took me aside. 'Elephants are like human beings, sahib,' he whispered. 'They like companionship. Don't leave her for too long.

Every evening before you sleep, talk to her. Tell her stories.'

To check again if the Maharaja had returned we drove to Belgania Palace. Formerly built to accommodate royal guests during the Durbar administration, it was now his home, as the original larger palace in the city had been turned into a college. Situated on a small hill with commanding views over Baripada, it was a big picturesque, colonnaded building, like a grand Florentine villa, the colour of burnt sienna, approached by a sweeping drive lined with flame-of-the-forest trees and jacaranda. An ageing *chowkidar* received us. We settled ourselves comfortably to start with, in easy chairs on a broad loggia, and then more nervously as a large, scarred Dobermann came and joined us. 'Brook, you bloody dog, get down,' a voice boomed as Brook began to take particular interest in one of my legs. A large, balding, unshaven man, dressed in a stained *kurta* and a *dhoti*, appeared. He looked tired. Black rings circled his eyes.

'Forgive me for keeping you waiting,' he said, 'but I was just finishing my *puja*.' With a smile he held out his hand and inquired our names. 'Patankar,' he said suspiciously. 'That's a Maratha name, isn't it?'

'That's right, sir,' Aditya replied proudly. 'I come from Gwalior.'

'Hmm,' he mused. 'Interesting. An Englishman and a Maratha. A friend and a foe. Two hundred years ago we suffered badly under the Maratha yoke. In fact, we joined forces with the Marquis Wellesley to stop you entering Bengal from the south. One of my ancestors, Rani Sumitra Devi, the adoptive mother of the *de facto* ruler of Mayurbhanj, was honoured by the British Government in recognition of her meritorious services. You must', he said pointedly to Aditya, with an amused twinkle in his eyes, 'have had a 41 very nostalgic journey through Orissa. Anyway, we are all friends now. Let us have tea. I will call my wife.'

It was the kind of tea that one longs for on journeys such as this; cucumber sandwiches, cream cakes and endless Benson and Hedges cigarettes (my usual brand which I had not smoked for two months). They were supplied kindly by his wife, a member of the Nepalese royal family, a beautifully coiffeured lady, smelling wonderfully of Worth perfume, wearing a pale, powder-blue sari and dashing diamanté-studded glasses. To begin with she was a little shy, but when our conversation turned to shopping she became very animated, eagerly praising the merits of Harrods and other famous stores.

'Where did you find your elephant?' the Maharaja asked.

'In a dreadful place called Daspalla,' I replied.

He laughed. 'Daspalla was famous for two things. The best elephants and the most stupid people.'

I told him of our journey through the Simlipals, which had once belonged to his family. On hearing of our exploits at Jenabil, his attitude was one of horror, telling us that our behaviour had been both foolish and irresponsible. However, he was grateful for the information and for what we had done.

'Sri Ram Naik always collected the resin from which I make my own incense. I knew him well. He was a splendid man.' As we were leaving, the Maharaja presented me with a plastic bag. I opened it. Inside were pieces of crystallized bark. 'This is resin,' he explained. 'Sri Ram Naik's last delivery.'

On the outskirts of Joshipur, we met up with two female elephants, the larger resembling an old and dusty tramp, dwarfing her little companion who hung on to her tail with her trunk. Both elephants were in poor condition – gaunt, almost skeletal. They stood listlessly, not bothering to brush away the flies that crawled over their eyes, from which dripped a white mucus. They greeted Tara, placing their trunks into her mouth. Standing beside them she shone – a beautiful Maharani attended by two dowdy maidservants.

'*Haathi* no good,' Bhim said disdainfully. 'Both no see.'

We stopped to talk with their mahouts, mendicants who were working their way south through Orissa. By November, they would return to Benares, where the elephants' owner lived, a rich *pandit* who kept a stable of forty elephants. The elder man sported a curling, white moustache, his greedy eyes never leaving Tara. He offered to sell us the smaller elephant for 60,000 rupees. As if to show her off, he yanked down viciously on the *ankush* which hung from a rusty pin, piercing one of her ears. In resignation, she simply shook her head slowly. He then offered half this price for Tara. His contemptuous proposal was met with howls of derision from us, and we moved on laughing, ridiculing his impudence.

Then it hit me. My laughter died. A feeling of cold dread swept over me. I had been offered a price: however absurd, it was still a price and for the first time I became aware of Tara's destiny. In that brief moment, the entire context of what I was doing changed. It was no longer the romantic ride on an elephant across India that I had dreamed up so flippantly – a whim to satisfy my ambitions. It was reality, however camouflaged by the colour and the beauty – it was there, hard and completely unchangeable. Tara was my responsibility, her future life lay in my hands and every step she took brought me nearer to that moment. I tried to force it into the back of my mind. But it was now there, hanging like a relentless black shadow.

Double Dipper

In a matter of a mile, the difference between Orissa and Bihar became visible. It was like suddenly parting the leaves on the edge of a rain forest and stepping into a scorched desert. Gone was the colour, the lushness, the laughter, the languid sensuality that manifested itself in Orissa, to be replaced by a harsh, suspicious and angry terrain. It showed in the quality of the tea, the sudden absence of fresh *paan*, the drabness of the *lunghis*, the condition of the villages and, above all, in the people. Our attitude changed accordingly. Bhim and Gokul became nervous and unsure of themselves.

Soon after we entered Bihar an incident occurred that exemplified this new feeling. An aggressive, stocky man, with a bald head that gleamed like a billiard ball in the sun, approached us driving a large loaded cart pulled by two bullocks. In an attempt to prevent the inevitable chaos, I steered Tara off the road and faced her away from the bullocks to allow them to pass as I had done in Orissa. He shouted at me angrily to get my elephant out of the way. I had already done this, but to avoid an unpleasant scene I moved a little further, at least two hundred yards off the road. He drove his bullocks forward, whipping them with a bamboo pole, and he had just come abreast of us when they panicked. Snorting with fear the bullocks raced along the road for a few yards, flew over a ten-foot drop to land in a muddy paddy field the other side, snapped their harness and made off quickly. Un-

44

impressed as I was with his character, I could not help but feel admiration for his driving skill. From a position with bullocks, cart and driver in mid-air, he landed the contraption like a seasoned jet pilot.

Unfortunately he did not reciprocate with admiration for Tara and me. He came stomping up the bank, gathering a few villagers on the way. 'This is my village and my road,' he spluttered furiously. 'Your elephant is a menace.'

'Excuse me, sir,' I interjected politely, 'this may be your village, but a road is built for the purposes of travel. Anybody can travel on it, including an elephant which, I would like to point out, is not a menace. If you recall, I moved off the road to let you pass.'

'Unless you give me compensation of five rupees I will impound your elephant,' he shouted. If he had been more civil and not insulted Tara, I would have paid gladly.

'How do you think you are going to impound my elephant?' I demanded angrily, flicking her behind the ear. She rolled her head and moved towards him. His eyes filled with alarm as this large beast loomed in front of him. He did not reply and we moved on.

Fortunately this feeling did not seem to be constant. At Majhgaon, a predominantly Muslim village, we were entertained royally by the elders, splendid old men in *dhotis* with long white beards. Delighted to see Tara, they crowded around her placing coins in her trunk, and even crushed paper money. Under the impression that the bank notes might contain something to eat, Tara investigated carefully, before dropping them despondently. Clearly, when she had been with Rajpath she had not received such riches.

One of the elders, the village tailor, took me into his shop over

which a sign proudly proclaimed IMAM TAILORS, MAJHGAON. PER-
FECT FITTING LADIES AND GENTS. GOD MAKE A MAN, WE MAKE
GENTLEMAN.

'If I may say so, sir,' he said, 'for an Englishman you are poorly
dressed.' Measuring my waistline, he presented me with a pair of
violet bell-bottom trousers and a matching shirt. 'Now,' he said,
eyeing me critically, 'you look like a gentleman.'

Indrajit and Khusto managed to find a quiet campsite that night.
To celebrate the halfway point of our journey we drank a great
deal of rum. Unsteady and feeling inexplicably maudlin, I made
my way over to where Tara was chained. I sat down in front of
her and a feeling of great sadness swept over me. It was then that
I knew I could not sell her. The two blind elephants, and the sight
of Tara when she had been with Rajpath, convinced me. I had to
find her a good home. She would never be a beggar again. I drank
more of the rum, wondering unrealistically if I could take her back
to England. Not to some concrete zoo but to a wonderful estate
where she could retire and live happily.

Many years ago the Duke of Devonshire had faced a similar
situation. He had met a lady who inquired what she could bring
back for him from her travels in India. He had replied jokingly,
'Ah, nothing less than an elephant.' To his astonishment, some
months later, an elephant duly arrived. It was kept in a large enclos-
ure in the grounds of his house in Chiswick developing an undying
passion for the gardener who put the animal to work. The elephant
brushed the paths with a broom held in its trunk, picked up grass
cuttings and watered the plants with the aid of a can. Its dexterity
and extraordinary intelligence did not end there. The Duke's
guests were entertained after dinner as the elephant pulled the cork

from the port bottle and handed it to the butler. Unfortunately, like many elephants, it developed a taste for alcohol and died of consumption in 1829.

Even as I realized I was fantasizing I felt a presence behind me. Aditya settled himself beside me and we gazed in silence at Tara.

'You know, Aditya,' I said eventually, 'I . . .'

'I know what you are thinking, Mark,' he interrupted. 'I feel the same. She has become part of me as well.'

'What are we going to do?' I asked desperately.

'I don't know. But Sonepur will be full of elephant experts, and I give you my word we will find a solution there.' Unable to shake off the feeling of unease, I went to bed.

Suddenly, late in the night, the fly of the tent was ripped open and Bhim tumbled drunkenly inside. 'No time left,' he shouted urgently. 'Journey soon over. Raja-sahib learn ride Mummy like good mahout. I watch today. No good.' He climbed on to Aditya's back, hooked his legs around his waist and proceeded to give a demonstration of toe movements. 'Daddy now Mummy,' he cried. 'Watch good, Raja-sahib, Bhim show you.' For the next half hour Aditya's legs were kneaded and crushed and his kneecaps grazed from the pressure of Bhim's horny toenails. Eventually Bhim exhausted himself and passed out.

'At least he's keen,' I remarked to Aditya as we carried him back to his tent.

'We were lucky to find him, Mark,' he replied. 'He cares.'

We climbed back into the tent. I was just falling asleep when a long, sinuous shape slid past the back of the tent, pressing against my head, which was wedged against the canvas. I sat bolt upright and shook Aditya. There was no need. He had felt it as well. I crawled quickly towards the front of the tent but Aditya grabbed me.

'Stay inside,' he said calmly, and yelled at Indrajit to investigate. A wild commotion followed. Then Indrajit poked his head in holding something long and bloody.

'*Nag*,' he said happily. 'I get it' – and he held up a five-foot cobra.

It was now getting cold in the mornings. We started later and later, waiting for the sun to rise, before facing the ice-cold water when bathing Tara. We travelled slowly northwards, passing people preparing to celebrate Dussehra, the festival which commemorates the victory of the warrior goddess, Durga, the consort of Shiva, over the buffalo-demon, Mahiasura. Drunkenly, they lay in the shade of large trees where hooch stalls had been set up. The powerful smell of *handia* or *raci*, as it is known in Bihar, hung in the hot air. With nose and trunk filled respectively with this irresistible temptation, both Bhim and Tara were finding it hard not to stop.

One evening we became part of a travelling circus. As we set up camp we were joined by a band of roving snake-charmers, delightful, gregarious rogues sartorially resplendent in bright yellow turbans decorated with feathers. Around their necks on beaded strings hung little leather pouches containing remedial herbs to cure snake bites. They carried their reptiles in circular, flat wicker boxes; six cobras, a krait and two lazy pythons.

Their presence attracted an even larger crowd than usual who watched spellbound as the cobras undulated hissing from the boxes and danced to the rhythm of little wooden drums. Bhim, not to be outdone by this slick showmanship, delighted the crowd further by coaxing a variety of sounds out of Tara both from her front and rear end.

Once out of the intoxication of the tribal belt, we crossed a landscape bleached white from the smoke of a large cement factory. Nearing the town of Chaibasa, we could almost have been in England, on a sharp, sunny, frosty morning. Each leaf and blade of grass was covered in a fine white powder that sparkled in the sunlight. To avoid this white wasteland we took a small back road. Spanning it was a tall wooden bridge under which a fast river flowed.

I urged Tara forward. After putting one foot cautiously down, she backed away. No inducement could make her cross it. Without me so much as uttering a command, she simply took over and wandered further up the river bank. After testing the depth she splashed over. On the other side we met a man who told us that the bridge was unsafe. It was now only used by pedestrians and cyclists. Three weeks ago a taxi driver had driven his vehicle half-way across and the timbers had suddenly splintered. Luckily he had managed to reverse to safety.

Similar incidents of an elephant's extreme cautiousness have been recorded. One was during the Sepoy rebellion in 1857. A general, riding an elephant, had been leading his army towards a bridge which spanned a deep ravine. Similarly, persuasion proved useless – the elephant refused to cross. The general, trusting his elephant's sagacity, had the structure examined, finding that the enemy had cut away the main supports.

The outskirts of Chaibasa reminded me of an English country village. In British days the town had been the centre of administration for south-eastern Bengal. We crossed green fields dotted 49

with clumps of giant mango and taller peepul trees. In the distance
the spire of a church trembled in the heat haze. Fine sturdy trees,
shading broad boulevards, gave relief from the hot sun and made
a passing snack for Tara. It must have been a pleasant place to be
stationed. But, according to the Bengal District *Gazetteers*, a Mr
Rickards wrote in 1854, 'There is everything in Chaibasa to make
a person want to leave it . . . it has not a single attraction.' And a
Dr Bell in 1868 added, 'those officers who have mastered the Ho
language and have become intimate with the people like this
station, but with the executive services of Bengal generally it is
regarded much in the light of a penal settlement.'

At a small bank we stopped to change travellers' cheques. The
manager could not understand why I wanted to travel through his
state. 'When God created Bihar, Mr Shand,' he told me, 'He was
in a very bad mood.'

The exquisite church, whose spire we had seen shimmering in
the distance, was of the Lutheran order and still retained its original
stained-glass windows. Built a hundred and eighty years ago, it
had an aura of dignity and simplicity, quite unlike its Roman Cath-
olic rival nearby, a modern atrocity glittering like a seaside fun
palace, complete with an ornate grotto-like shrine in which the
Virgin Mary was lit by red and blue lights. Inside, converted tribals
polished an already gleaming marble floor in which the giant gem-
studded cross was reflected.

As we left Chaibasa for Seraikella, where we had been invited
to stay by the Raja, we stopped to watch a game of cricket played
by some college boys. A fine pull through mid-wicket sent the ball
skimming towards us. It stopped just in front of Tara. She eyed
this foreign object with interest and then cautiously rolled it around

with the tip of her trunk. Satisfied the ball was inedible she stamped on it, embedding it into the hard ground. A group of players had by now run over. They stood in front of her silently, undecided about what they should do. One of them, braver than the rest, stepped forward.

'Excuse me, sir,' he asked politely. 'Um, could we be having our ball back. It is the only one we have.'

'Of course, I am sorry,' I said confidently, commanding Tara to move back and dig out the ball. Nothing happened. She stood firmly in place, flapping her ears. I repeated the command. Again she ignored me. I dismounted, rapped her on the trunk and dug the ball out myself. 'Here you are,' I said embarrassed and furious at her behaviour, tossing it back to them.

'Maybe your elephant is liking playing cricket,' one of them suggested with a laugh.

'Oh, yes, she is really very clever.' Taking the ball back, I tossed it at Tara. She did nothing. There was a soft thud as it hit her in the centre of her trunk. I repeated the manoeuvre to no avail. Eventually, I threw the ball back to the players. 'She's just out of practice.'

'You old bag,' I whispered to her. 'You let me down. You may be a slow learner, but that was pathetic. After all you are an Indian elephant. You should bloody well know how to play cricket.'

My accusations were a little unfair. Although an elephant is slow to learn, with practice it will repeat almost anything faultlessly, just like the amazing elephant cricket team, the famous animal trainer John Grindl of Bertram Mills's Circus succeeded in coaching. In his book *Elephants* Richard Carrington records that a pair of elephants would take up their stations at opposite ends of the arena, one with a cap and pads and holding a bat in his trunk, while the other bowled. On either side four or five others were ranged as fielders. At the word of command the bowler threw the ball down the pitch and the batsman took a ferocious swipe at it with his trunk. More often than not the bat connected and the elephant would plod down the arena for a run. Meanwhile, one of the fielding elephants would stop the ball and throw it at the stumps. It took Grindl several months of patient effort to perfect his act. He began by standing in front of the batting elephant, grasping both bat and trunk in his own hands. Another man would then bowl the ball and Grindl would guide the elephant's trunk to hit it. After many hundreds of attempts, the elephant grasped the idea and hit the ball on its own. A similar technique was employed with the bowler and fielders. Thereafter there was no holding them, and they would play the game with enormous enthusiasm.

In the blistering heat the road to Seraikella stretched before us unendingly. My stiffness had now almost vanished. Hard yellow calluses decorated the ends of my toes, but the sides of my legs were blue from bruising, where Tara's great ears hammered ceaselessly against them.

I was beginning to feel comfortable with her and perhaps she with me. My self-consciousness was vanishing and I barked at her fiercely when she tried to steal paddy or slow down unnecessarily. Considering she was supposed to be a Koonki elephant, she moved remarkably slowly and I had continually to work on her to achieve an even pace. Gradually the habits of a beggar elephant were dying and I felt she was acquiring a new pride.

En route we picked up our first hitchhiker, a young tribal who displayed great excitement on seeing a large dead snake in the middle of the road.

'What on earth was that all about?' I asked Aditya.

'Our friend has expressed a wish that the snake would come alive and bite him.'

'What!'

'He believes that it belongs to the lowest caste of snakes. It is, in fact, an untouchable. Therefore once our friend bears this mark, all other snakes will avoid him.'

We dropped off our logical companion on the outskirts of Seraikella. By the time we entered the town it was dark. Power cuts added to the confusion as Tara picked her way with uncanny sureness, waving her trunk constantly as a blind man uses his stick. Elephants are short-sighted animals and rely on their remarkable proboscis to sense rather than see their way. At one moment we padded silently in a complete black-out, the next we found ourselves in the middle of a busy, brightly lit street. At the sudden sight of this huge animal, bicyclists fell off their machines and passers-by shouted in alarm. A man on a brand-new red Vespa suddenly swung out in front of us.

'Welcome to Seraikella. I am relation of the King of the princely state of Seraikella. Excuse me,' he added with an embarrassed laugh, 'that is not quite correct. I am relation of the ex-King of the ex-princely state of Seraikella. Please follow me.' Guided by this curious outrider, we made our way through a maze of twisting streets, eventually arriving at a pair of large wooden gates, which were thrown open.

Waiting in the palace courtyard were the Raja, a plump, bespectacled man, and his younger brother, tall and elegant, who spoke 53 perfect English. The Raja performed a small *puja* and anointed Tara's feet. Then he pointed to a huge, ancient frangipani tree, the roots of which were embedded in the wall, almost as if they had started life together. He told us we could chain Tara there. Bhim made a closer inspection of the tree and shook his head.

'Excuse me, sir,' I said to the Raja, 'my mahout does not think this tree is strong enough. I am afraid my elephant will destroy it.'

However much I appealed, the Raja insisted that it was the right place, telling me that the tree was five hundred years old, sturdy and particularly auspicious to the family, making it essential that Ganesh should rest there. As we followed the Raja and his brother, I heard the crack of the first branch being snapped off contemptuously.

Through a narrow porchway Aditya and I were led on to a spacious lawn where the Raja suggested we pitch our tents. He then disappeared to watch television and we settled down to talk with his brother.

I was interested to hear that Seraikella and Kharsawan, a neighbouring principality, were the only two states in all of British India that were never required to pay taxes to the British. In 1793 a friendship treaty had been signed between the ruling Raja and the East India Company in recognition of Seraikella's protection of the Company's salt industry by preventing salt smugglers from entering the kingdom. Aditya was more pleased to hear that the treaty was also granted in connection with the help that the Raja's armies had supplied to the British against the ferocity of the Maratha invasion.

Then the Raja's brother spoke about the Chhow dance. Serai-kella is famous for this dance, which is performed in honour of

Lord Shiva. Now, the Chhow is almost completely organized and financed by the Raja's brother, himself a leading dancer, who has taken his troupe to London, Paris, Rome, Munich and New York. All the dancers are male. All wear masks. The choreography requires that the dancers should express the moods through the limbs alone, since if the mask is discarded, the face then becomes the major focus of attraction. The Raja's brother had arranged for us to see a performance – a dress-rehearsal only, he apologized – in the village of Govindpur.

We left the boys to put up the tents and drove with the Raja's brother to the village. In the mud courtyard of a farmer's simple home the dancers were dressing for the performance. Lying incongruously among the terracotta milk urns and the cows were big steel costume trunks covered in colourful stickers from grand hotels in Italy, England, Germany and other European countries. The dancers, all clad in costumes of exquisite finery, coloured their hands and the soles of their feet with vermilion, their faces now obscured by painted plaster masks. Surrounded by cattle stalls and lit by kerosene lamps, we were entertained to a superb display of the Chhow dance. Through the movement of the feet alone, as they leapt, turned and gyrated to the rhythms of the drums and other instruments, the dancers suggested not only the more traditional legends but also brought to life their own humble, daily occupations, such as fishing and hunting.

In the Peacock Dance, the young dancer managed to convey all the vanity of this colourful bird by moving only the upper part of his body to emphasize the extended fan of tail feathers. Another, dressed as a bee, seemed actually to hover, vibrating the sequinned wings attached to his back, as he darted around yet another dancer

55

dressed as a flower. Sometimes, in this particular dance, the wings are made of stone, so one can imagine the stamina required.

What impressed me most was the avid concentration of the village audience, particularly among the small boys watching. I have found many times, when attending a dance in other remote areas, the audience's concentration centred rather on the tourist or the click of the camera. But here Aditya and I were totally ignored. The small boys' eyes were glued to the scene in front of them and, like young critics, they applauded a fine move or criticized a mistake.

On returning to our tents on the palace lawn, we discovered the boys in a state of considerable excitement. They were all vying for the attentions of the maidservant to the Raja's wife, a deliciously attractive young woman, who was heartlessly teasing them. All through the evening, I had received reports of how she had given Gokul and Khusto a 'dipper' and then Indrajit a 'double dipper'. Even Bhim, distracted for a change from booze and Tara, joined in, announcing firmly, to the derision of the others, that she obviously preferred older men, as she had given him a 'triple dipper'. It all sounded somewhat pornographic until Aditya discovered that a 'dipper' was nothing more than a wink. The whole game was later put to an end by the Raja's wife, who banished the girl to her room.

Early the next morning I fetched Tara for her bath. Where once had stood a five-hundred-year-old frangipani tree and a wall now lay a mass of splintered branches and crumbling stonework, occupied by an elephant with an innocent expression on her face. I unshackled her and headed for the river. Luckily, as it was the first time I had taken her alone to bathe, she was very quiet, almost lackadaisical, and behaved impeccably, but I was still very much on guard against her sudden pranks.

The River Kharkai was wonderfully clean and swirled its way across smooth, round boulders, having started its journey at the waterfall at Barehipani in the Simlipals. We waded into the cool, refreshing water. Tara sank slowly down on her knees, allowing me to dismount, and then rolled over happily on to her side. For an hour, I scrubbed her from the tip of her trunk to the end of her tail. Exhausted, I stretched out on her stomach and took the sun while she lay quietly, half submerged, beneath me. Around us a group of men went about their morning ablutions without concern, speaking softly to avoid disturbing us.

I rode her back to the palace, where I found a forlorn-looking Bhim standing nervously behind the Raja, who was surveying the damage. I apologized profusely. Although I could see he was both astounded and quite upset, he assured me that it really did not matter. In another five hundred years, he told me, another tree would stand there. After all, he added, it would be something that he could tell his grandchildren.

He garlanded Tara with flowers from the fallen frangipani tree and we left. On our way out I noticed Indrajit looking anxiously at a high window in the turret of the palace. It opened slowly and a slim hand darted out dropping a single orange marigold. Indrajit picked it up and placed it carefully behind his ear. 'Double dipper,' he said happily. 'She like me the best.'

PENGUIN 60s

ISABEL ALLENDE · *Voices in My Ear*
NICHOLSON BAKER · *Playing Trombone*
LINDSEY BAREHAM · *The Little Book of Big Soups*
KAREN BLIXEN · *From the Ngong Hills*
DIRK BOGARDE · *Coming of Age*
ANTHONY BURGESS · *Childhood*
ANGELA CARTER · *Lizzie Borden*
CARLOS CASTANEDA · *The Sorcerer's Ring of Power*
ELIZABETH DAVID · *Peperonata and Other Italian Dishes*
RICHARD DAWKINS · *The Pocket Watchmaker*
GERALD DURRELL · *The Pageant of Fireflies*
RICHARD ELLMANN · *The Trial of Oscar Wilde*
EPICURUS · *Letter on Happiness*
MARIANNE FAITHFULL · *Year One*
KEITH FLOYD · *Hot and Spicy Floyd*
ALEXANDER FRATER · *Where the Dawn Comes Up Like Thunder*
ESTHER FREUD · *Meeting Bilal*
JOHN KENNETH GALBRAITH · *The Culture of Contentment*
ROB GRANT AND DOUG NAYLOR · *Scenes from the Dwarf*
ROBERT GRAVES · *The Gods of Olympus*
JANE GRIGSON · *Puddings*
SOPHIE GRIGSON · *From Sophie's Table*
KATHARINE HEPBURN · *Little Me*
SUSAN HILL · *The Badness Within Him*
ALAN HOLLINGHURST · *Adventures Underground*
BARRY HUMPHRIES · *Less is More Please*
HOWARD JACOBSON · *Expulsion from Paradise*
P. D. JAMES · *The Girl Who Loved Graveyards*
STEPHEN KING · *Umney's Last Case*
LAO TZU · *Tao Te Ching*
DAVID LEAVITT · *Chips Is Here*

PENGUIN 60s

LAURIE LEE · *To War in Spain*
PATRICK LEIGH FERMOR · *Loose as the Wind*
ELMORE LEONARD · *Trouble at Rindo's Station*
DAVID LODGE · *Surprised by Summer*
BERNARD MAC LAVERTY · *The Miraculous Candidate*
SHENA MACKAY · *Cloud-Cuckoo-Land*
NORMAN MAILER · *The Dressing Room*
PETER MAYLE · *Postcards from Summer*
JAN MORRIS · *Scenes from Havian Life*
BLAKE MORRISON · *Camp Cuba*
VLADIMIR NABOKOV · *Now Remember*
REDMOND O'HANLON · *A River in Borneo*
STEVEN PINKER · *Thinking in Tongues*
CRAIG RAINE · *Private View*
CLAUDIA RODEN · *Ful Medames and Other Vegetarian Dishes*
HELGE RUBINSTEIN · *Chocolate Parfait*
SIMON SCHAMA · *The Taking of the Bastille*
WILL SELF · *The Rock of Crack As Big As the Ritz*
MARK SHAND · *Elephant Tales*
NIGEL SLATER · *30-Minute Suppers*
RICK STEIN · *Fresh from the Sea*
LYTTON STRACHEY · *Florence Nightingale*
PAUL THEROUX · *Slow Trains to Simla*
COLIN THUBRON · *Samarkand*
MARK TULLY · *Beyond Purdah*
LAURENS VAN DER POST · *Merry Christmas, Mr Lawrence*
MARGARET VISSER · *More than Meets the Eye*
GAVIN YOUNG · *Something of Samoa*

and

Thirty Obituaries from Wisden · SELECTED BY MATTHEW ENGEL

READ MORE IN PENGUIN

For complete information about books available from Penguin and how to order them, please write to us at the appropriate address below. Please note that for copyright reasons the selection of books varies from country to country.

IN THE UNITED KINGDOM: Please write to *Dept. EP, Penguin Books Ltd, Bath Road, Harmondsworth, Middlesex UB7 0DA.*

IN THE UNITED STATES: Please write to *Consumer Sales, Penguin USA, P.O. Box 999, Dept. 17109, Bergenfield, New Jersey 07621-0120.* VISA and MasterCard holders call 1-800-253-6476 to order Penguin titles.

IN CANADA: Please write to *Penguin Books Canada Ltd, 10 Alcorn Avenue, Suite 300, Toronto, Ontario M4V 3B2.*

IN AUSTRALIA: Please write to *Penguin Books Australia Ltd, P.O. Box 257, Ringwood, Victoria 3134.*

IN NEW ZEALAND: Please write to *Penguin Books (NZ) Ltd, Private Bag 102902, North Shore Mail Centre, Auckland 10.*

IN INDIA: Please write to *Penguin Books India Pvt Ltd, 706 Eros Apartments, 56 Nehru Place, New Delhi 110 019.*

IN THE NETHERLANDS: Please write to *Penguin Books Netherlands bv, Postbus 3507, NL-1001 AH Amsterdam.*

IN GERMANY: Please write to *Penguin Books Deutschland GmbH, Metzlerstrasse 26, 60594 Frankfurt am Main.*

IN SPAIN: Please write to *Penguin Books S. A., Bravo Murillo 19, 1° B, 28015 Madrid.*

IN ITALY: Please write to *Penguin Italia s.r.l., Via Felice Casati 20, I-20124 Milano.*

IN FRANCE: Please write to *Penguin France S. A., 17 rue Lejeune, F-31000 Toulouse.*

IN JAPAN: Please write to *Penguin Books Japan, Ishikiribashi Building, 2-5-4, Suido, Bunkyo-ku, Tokyo 112.*

IN GREECE: Please write to *Penguin Hellas Ltd, Dimocritou 3, GR-106 71 Athens.*

IN SOUTH AFRICA: Please write to *Longman Penguin Southern Africa (Pty) Ltd, Private Bag X08, Bertsham 2013.*